This book belongs to:

_____

Newest Member of the
Color Me Successful Team

Animal Trainer

Archeologist

Army Officer

Artist

Astronaut

Athlete

Chef

Cosmetologist

Dancer

Dentist

Doctor

Fashion
Designer

Firefighter

Gymnast

Jockey

Judge

Model

Movie Director

Musician

News Anchor

Olympic
Fencer

Photographer

Pilot

Police
Officer

Police Station

Politician

Postal Carrier

Race Car Driver

Referee

Scientist

Writer

COLOR ME SUCCESSFUL ACTIVITIES

IMAGINE ME

In the space below, imagine yourself being successful in any career you want. Draw a picture of yourself in that career and below it write your name and Future _____(career name)
Ex: Lisa, Future Doctor

A mail carrier delivers mail or packages to businesses or homes.

Your job is to help the mail carrier get the mail to its destination.

Girls can grow up and be anything!

Match the descriptions with the correct career.

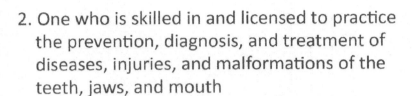

1. A person who designs, builds, or maintains engines, machines, or public works

2. One who is skilled in and licensed to practice the prevention, diagnosis, and treatment of diseases, injuries, and malformations of the teeth, jaws, and mouth

3. A person who sells or grows for sale flowers

4. A person who flies or is qualified to fly an aircraft or spacecraft

5. A person trained in gymnastics

6. Journalists who inform the public by reporting news stories and events happening on a local, national, and international level

Pilot

News Anchor

Gymnast

Engineer

Florist

Dentist

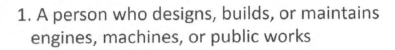

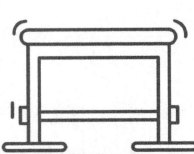

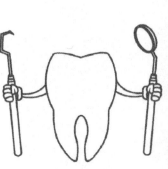

STEP INTO THE AUTHOR'S CHAIR

Writers or Authors begin with an idea and then build on it.
They develop characters, problems, and write stories to solve them.
Use the space below to write a story of your own!

ORDER UP!

Chefs are like artists in the kitchen.
Here's your chance to design a delicious meal and dessert.
Write or draw your meal.
Include a main dish, sides and of course....DESSERT

Main Dish

Notes:

Sides

Dessert

Draw your Meal

Made in the USA
Middletown, DE
07 May 2021